Halloween Coloring Book

By

S.B. Nozaz

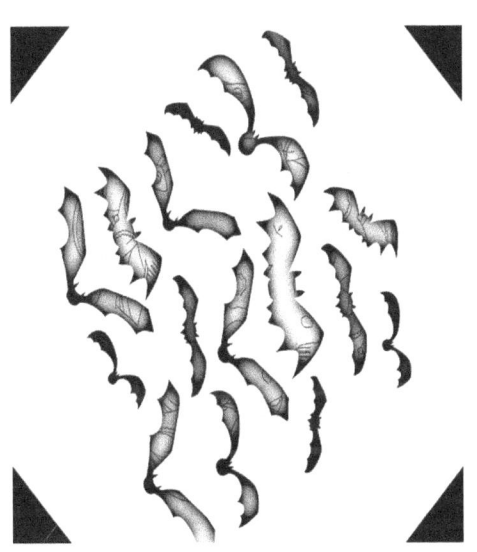

Copyright © 2015 by S.B. Nozaz

Introduction

Halloween is a great fun time for children. This fun time can stimulate their imagination about many kinds of Halloween symbols such as goblins, zombies, Dracula, ghosts, , witches, bats, black cats, pumpkins and their special characters. S.B. Nozaz has created this book for everyone who love and would like to enjoy Halloween more and more. Let's try it.

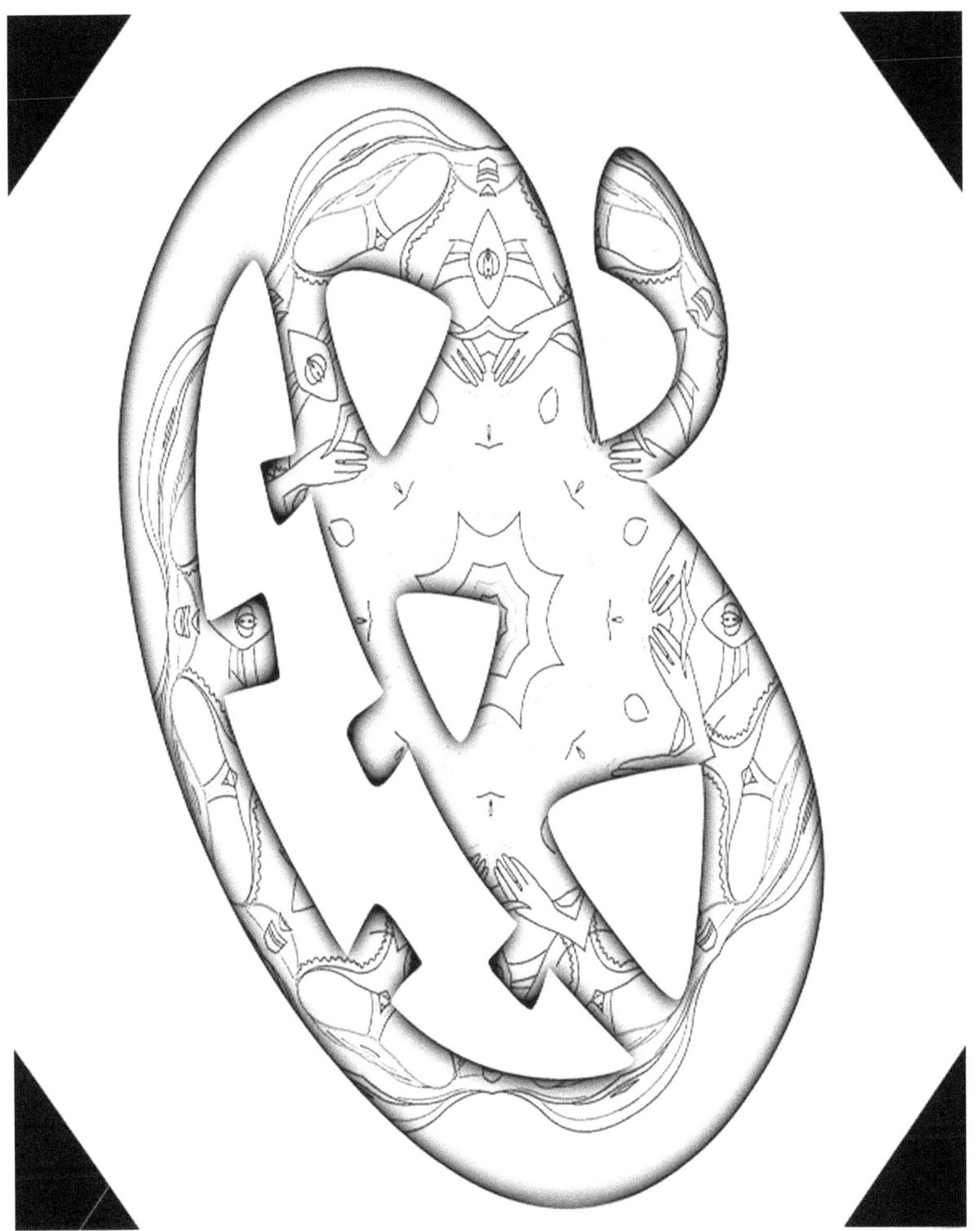

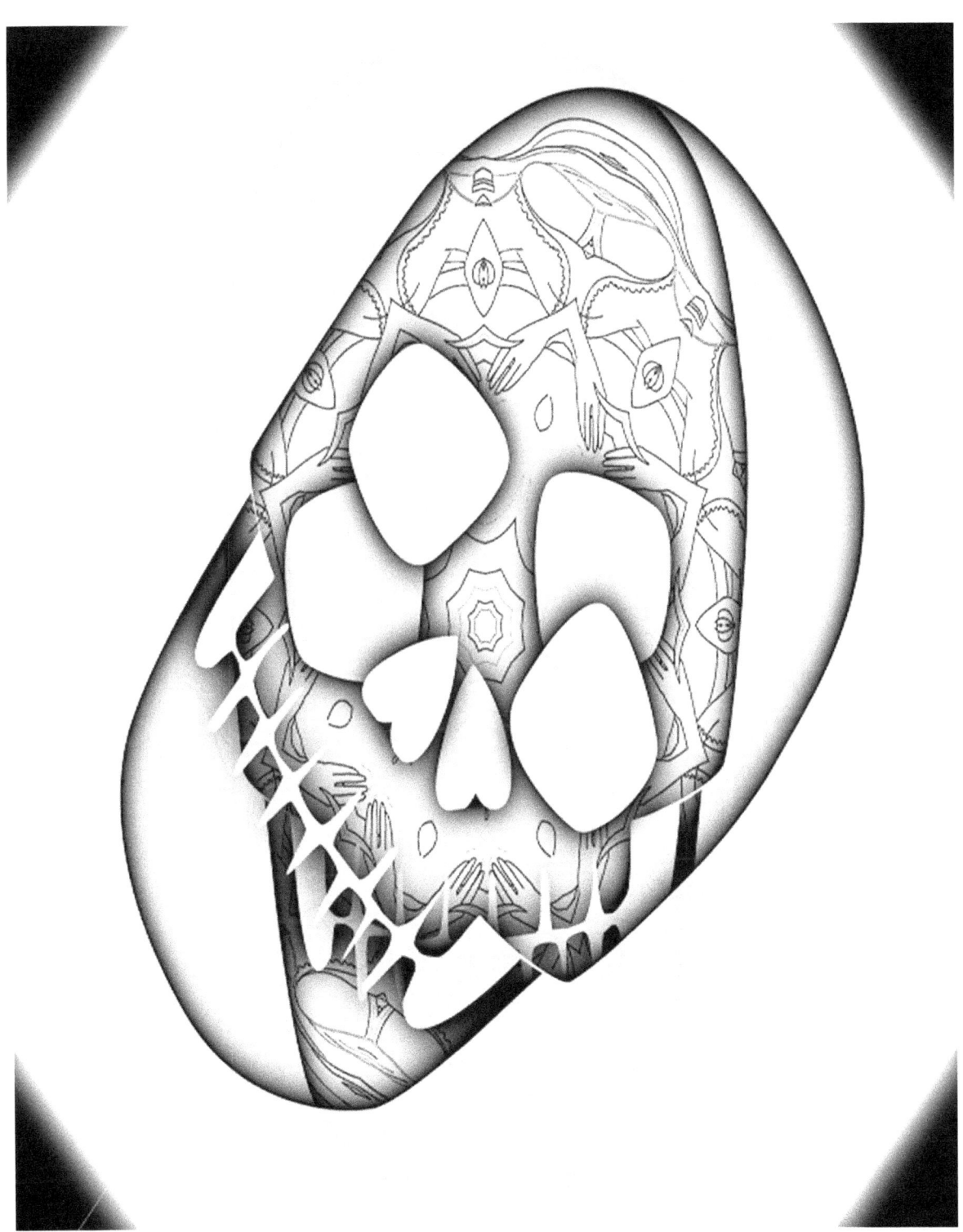

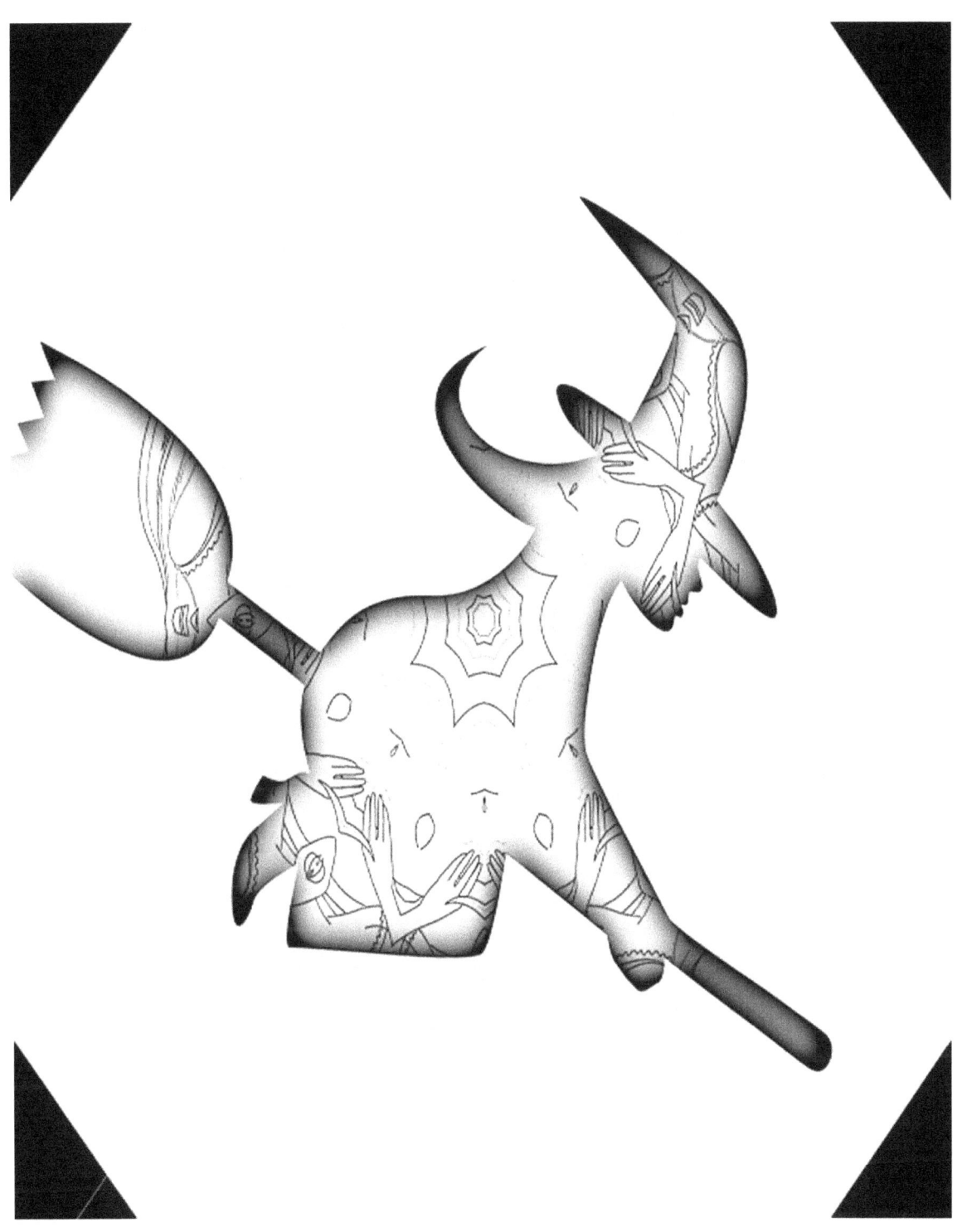

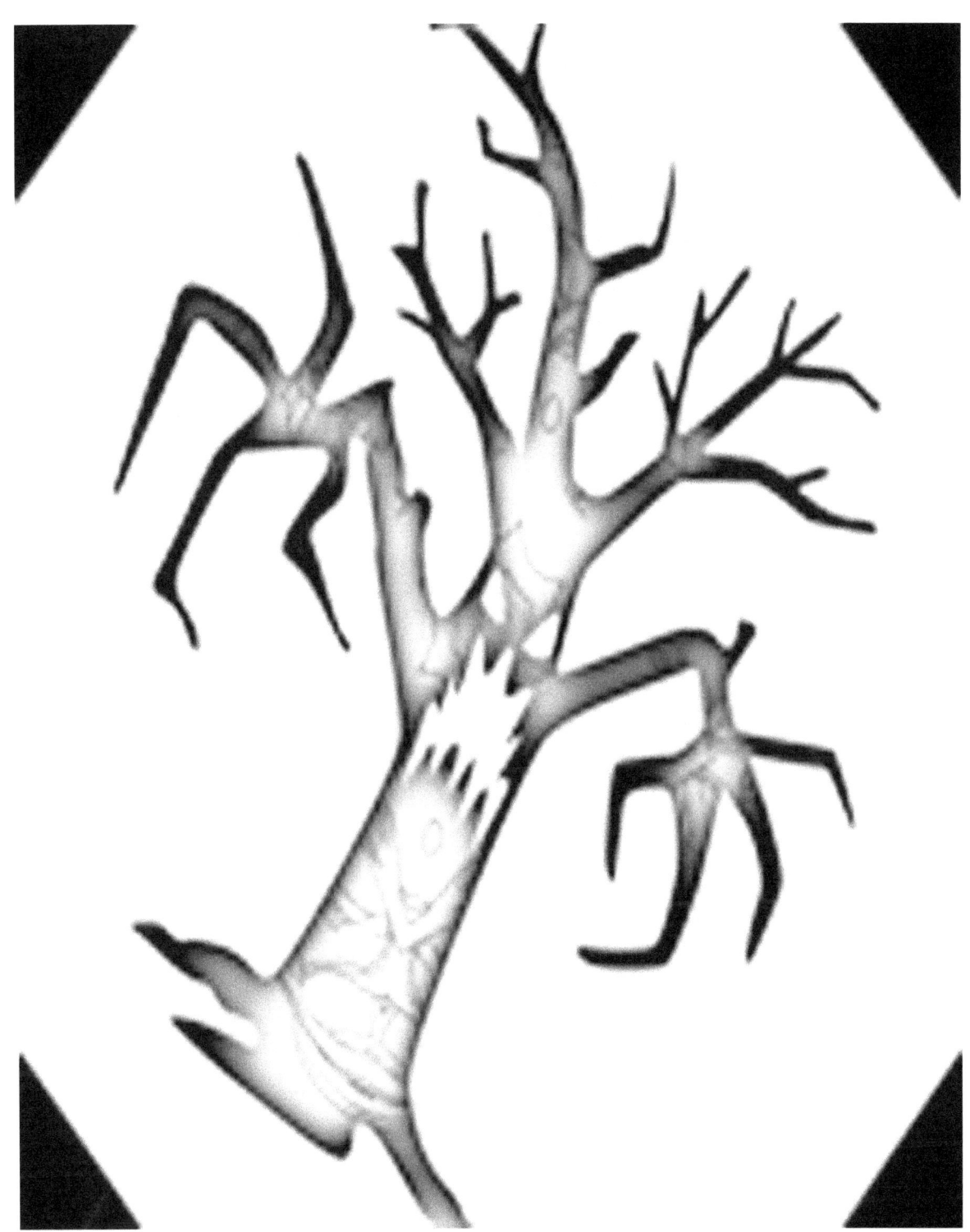

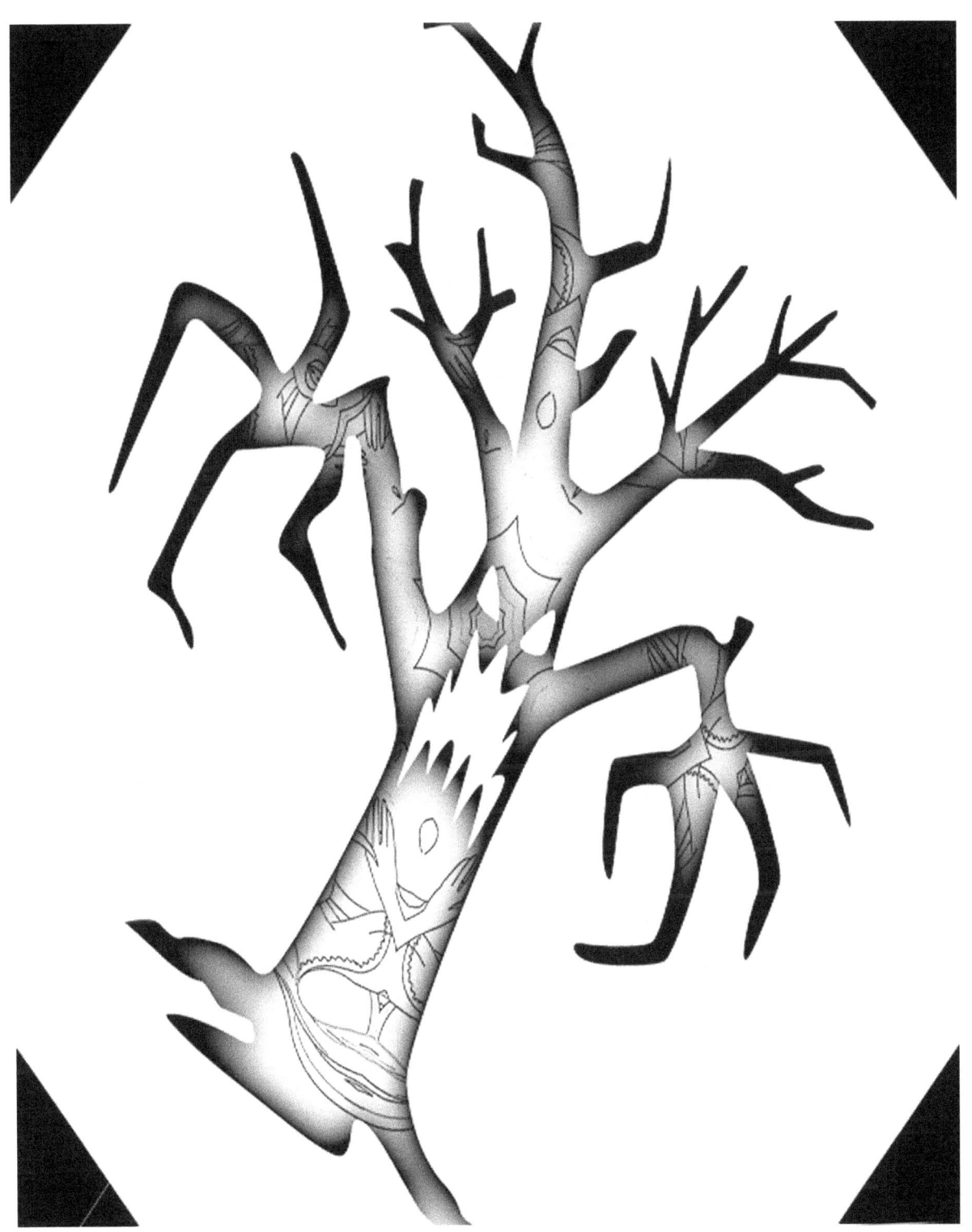

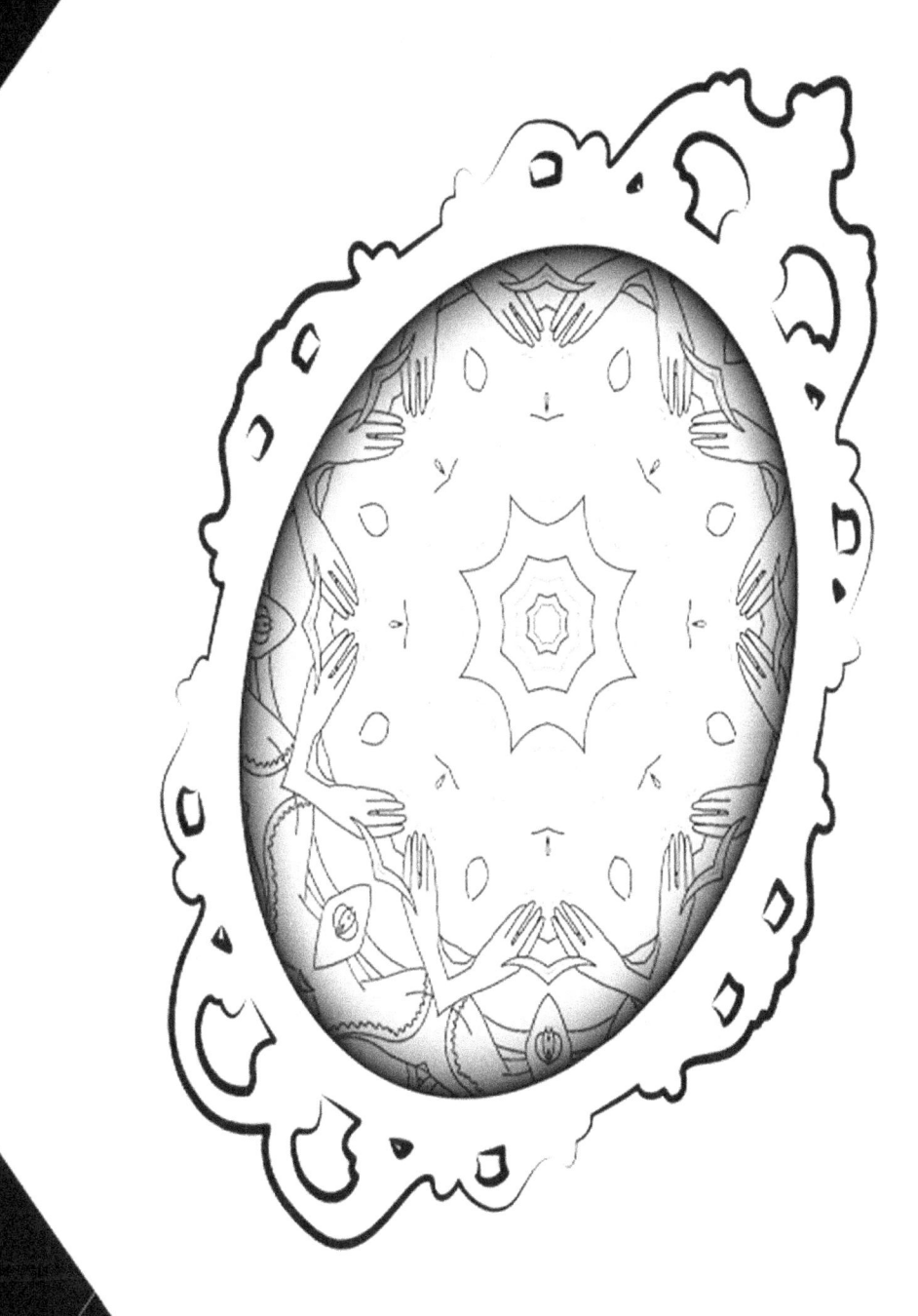

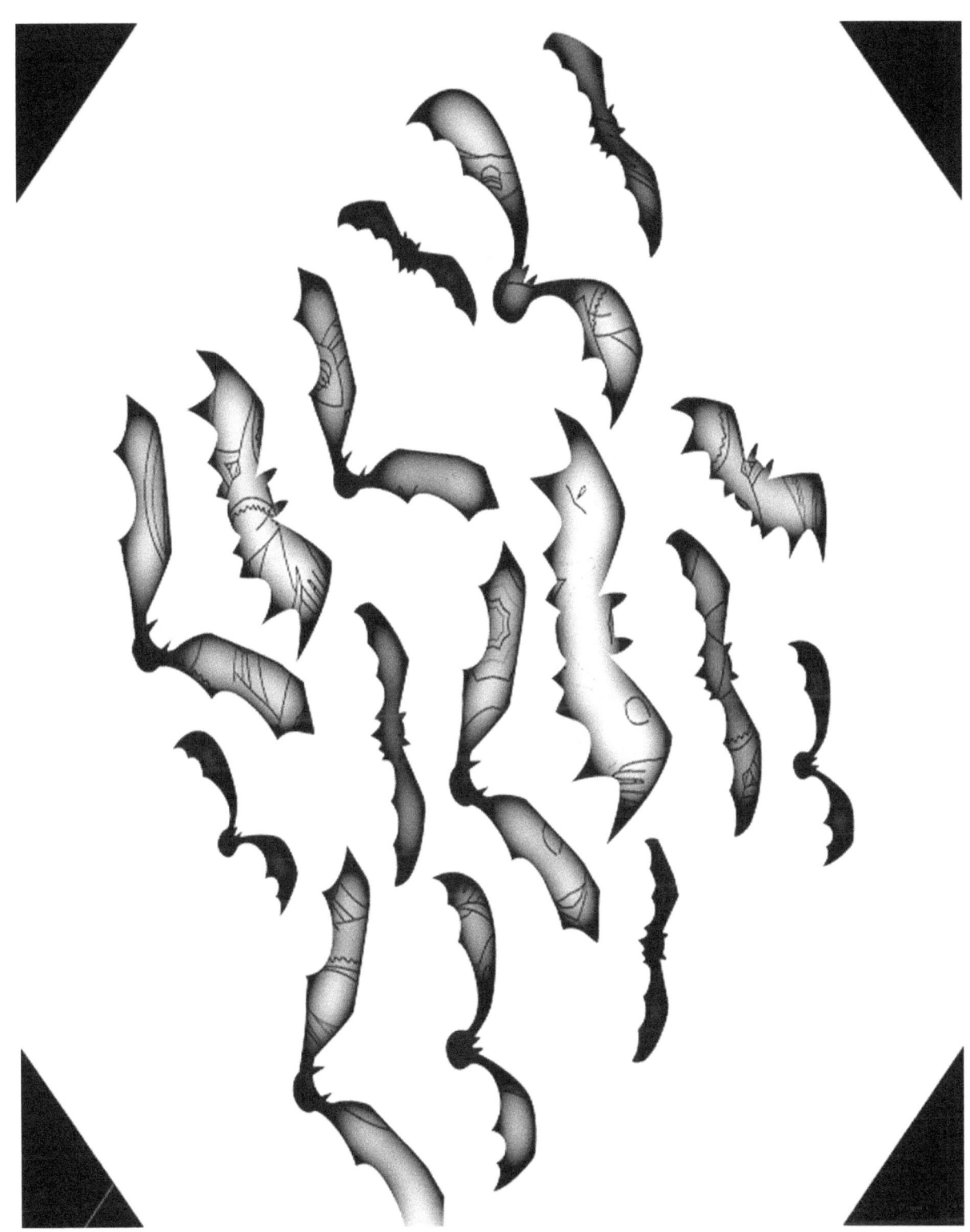

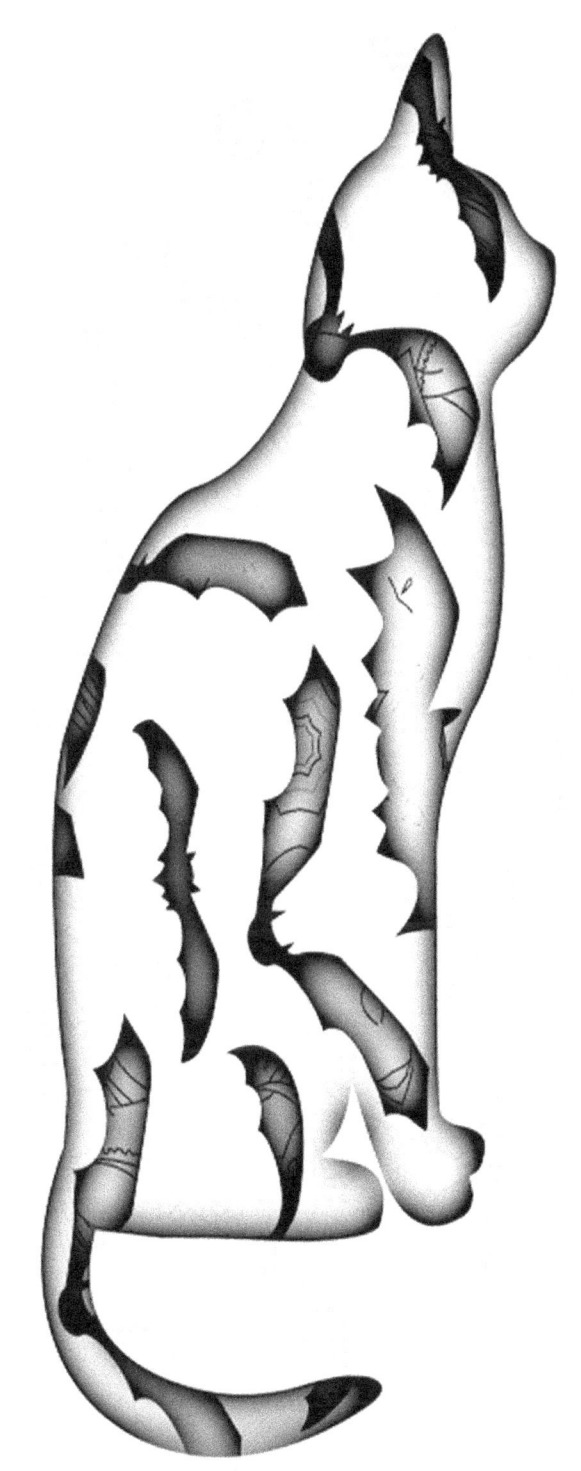

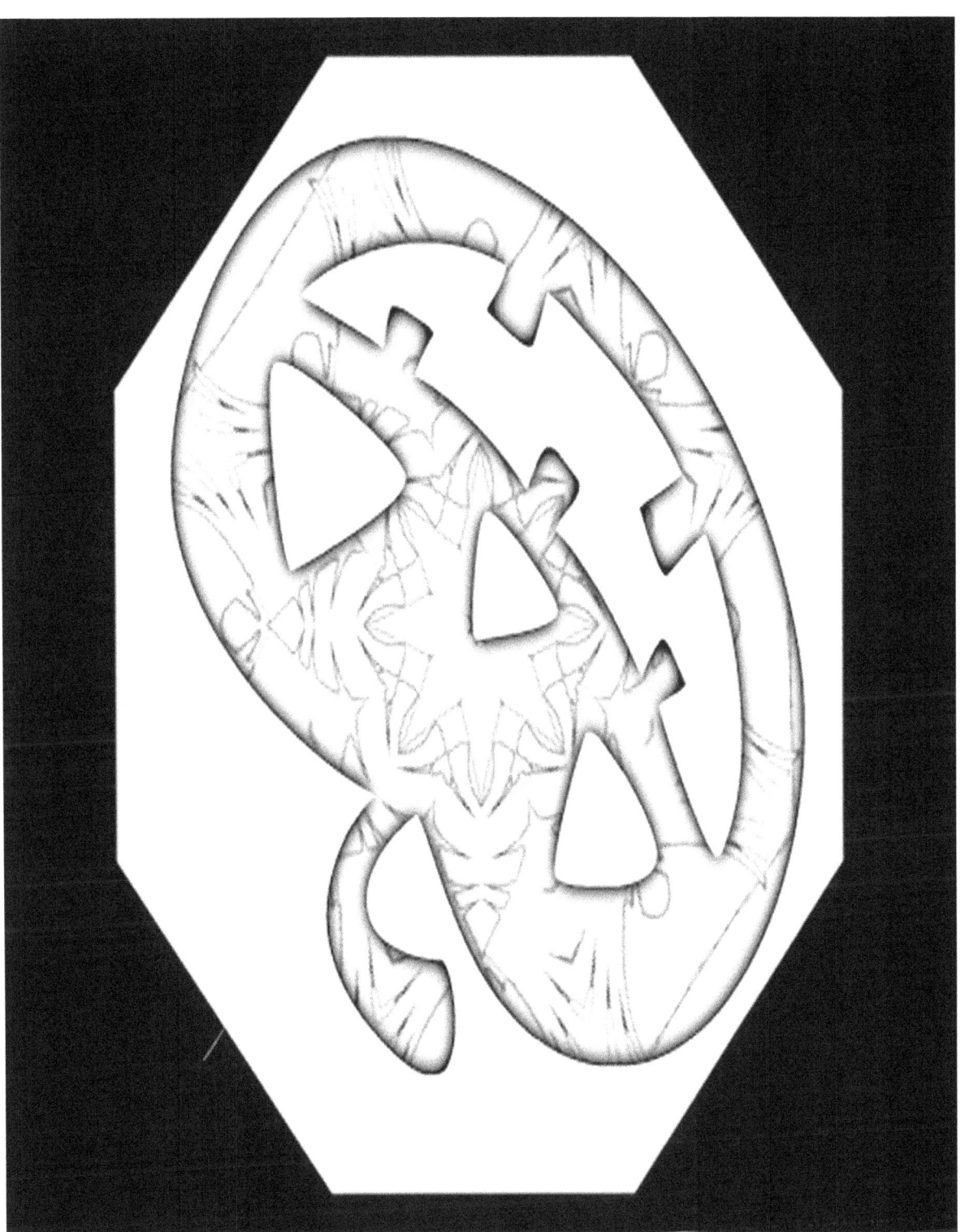

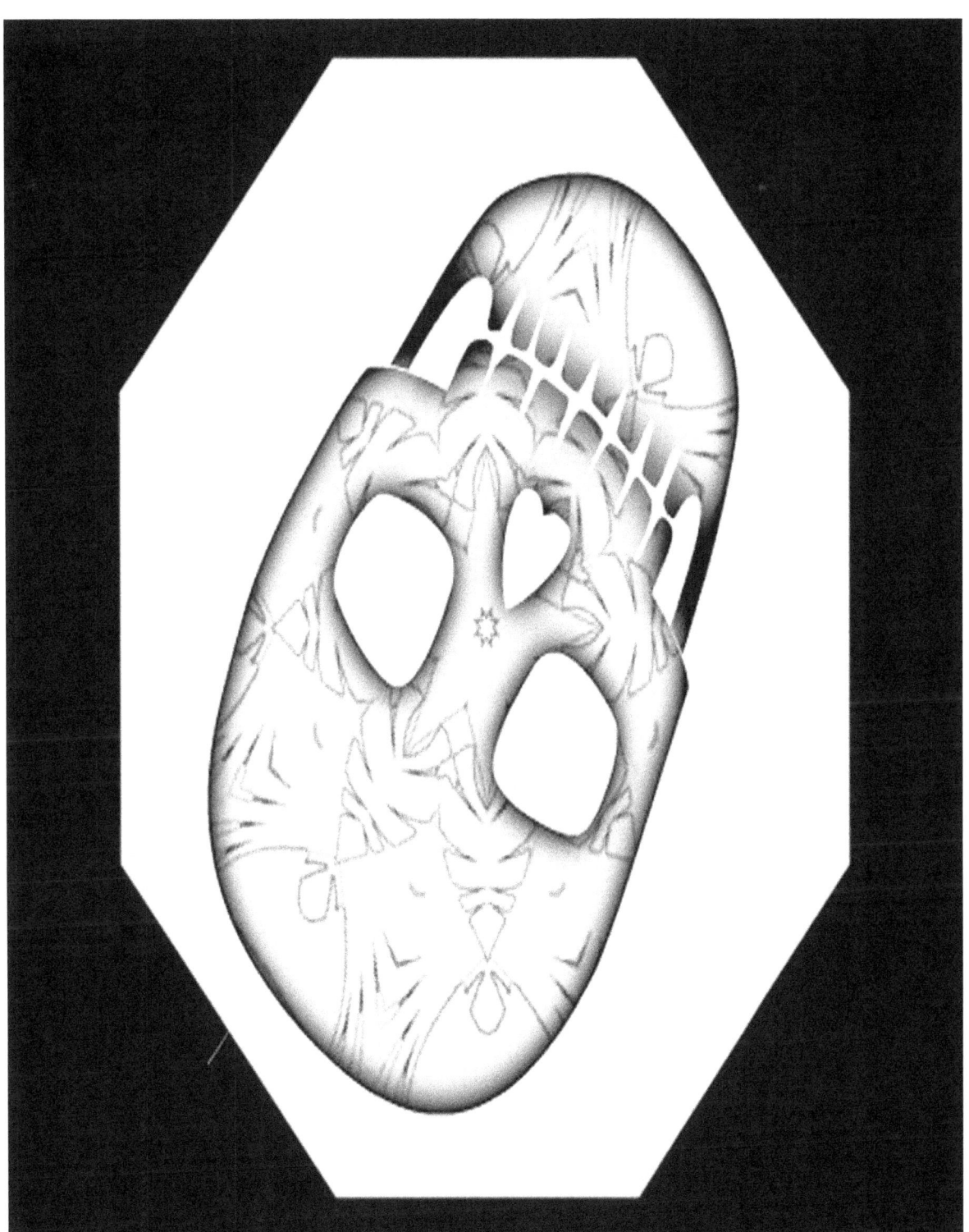

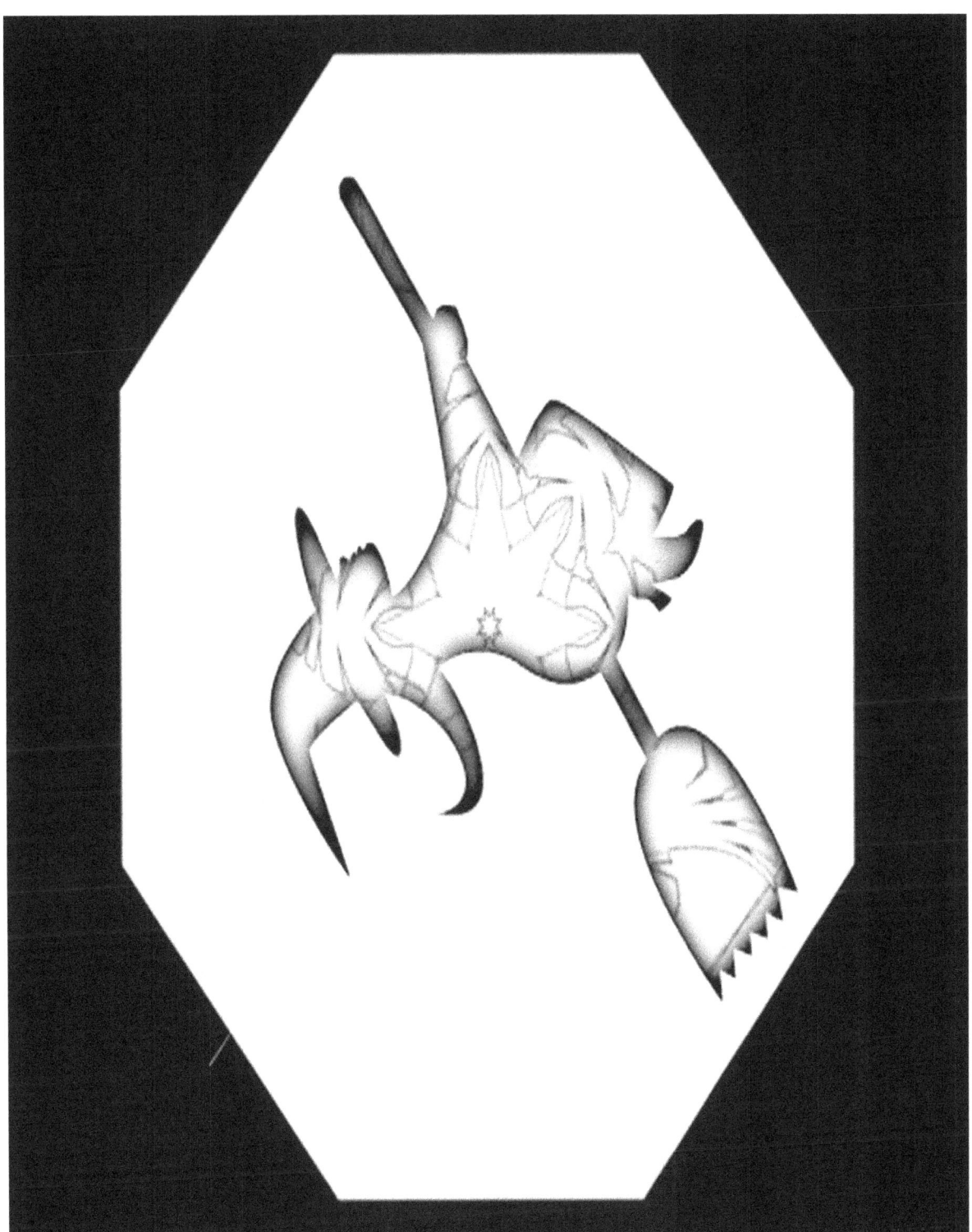

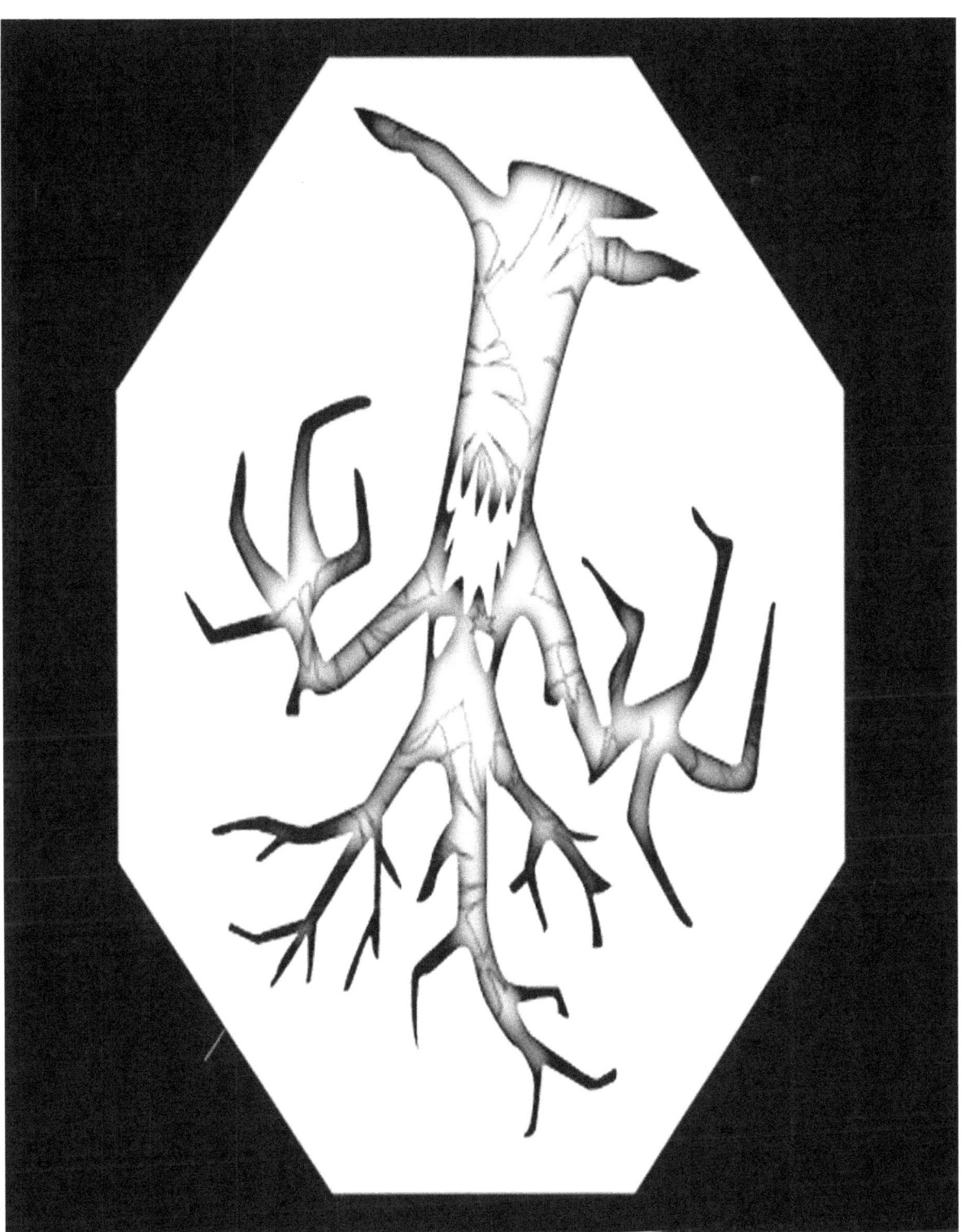

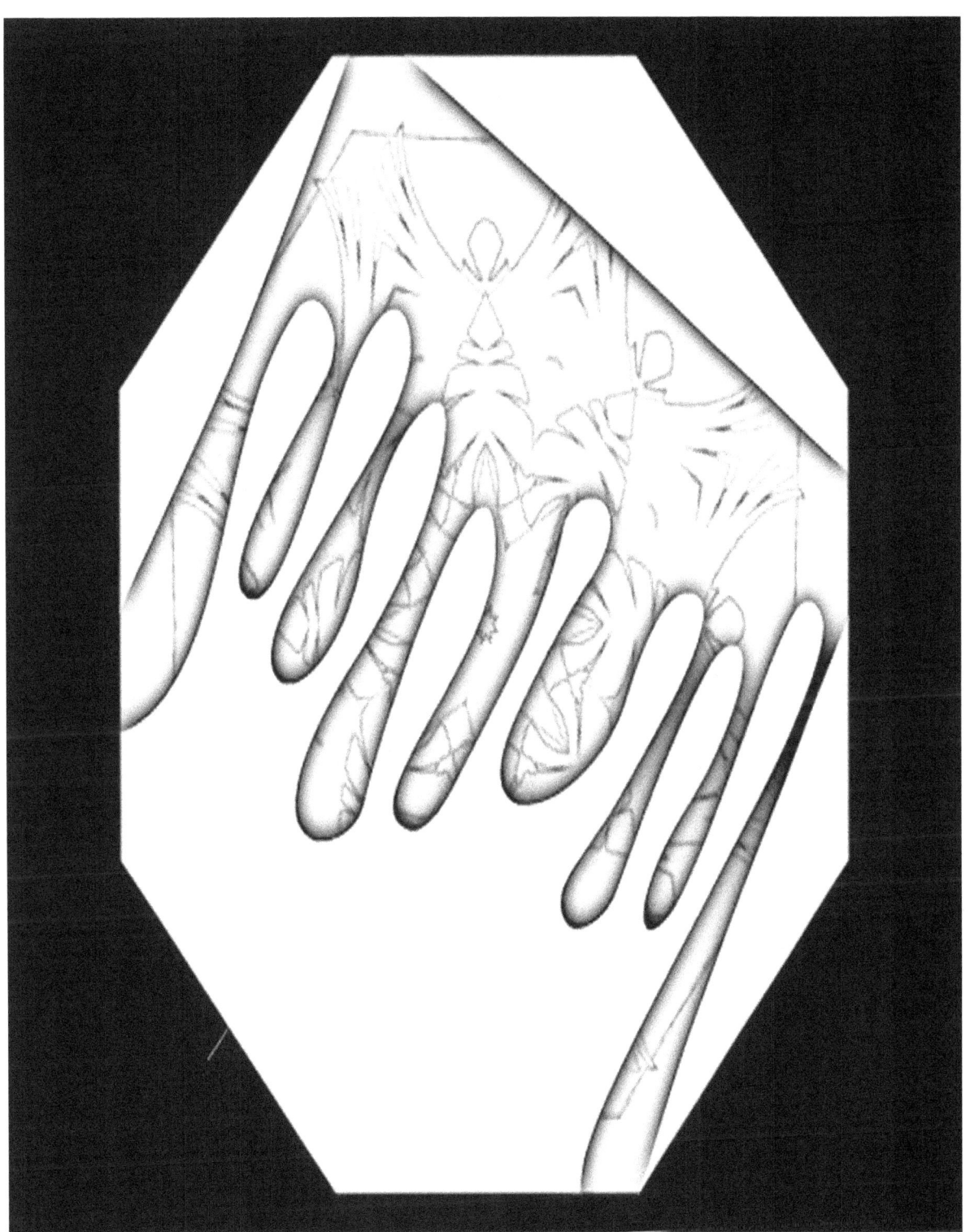

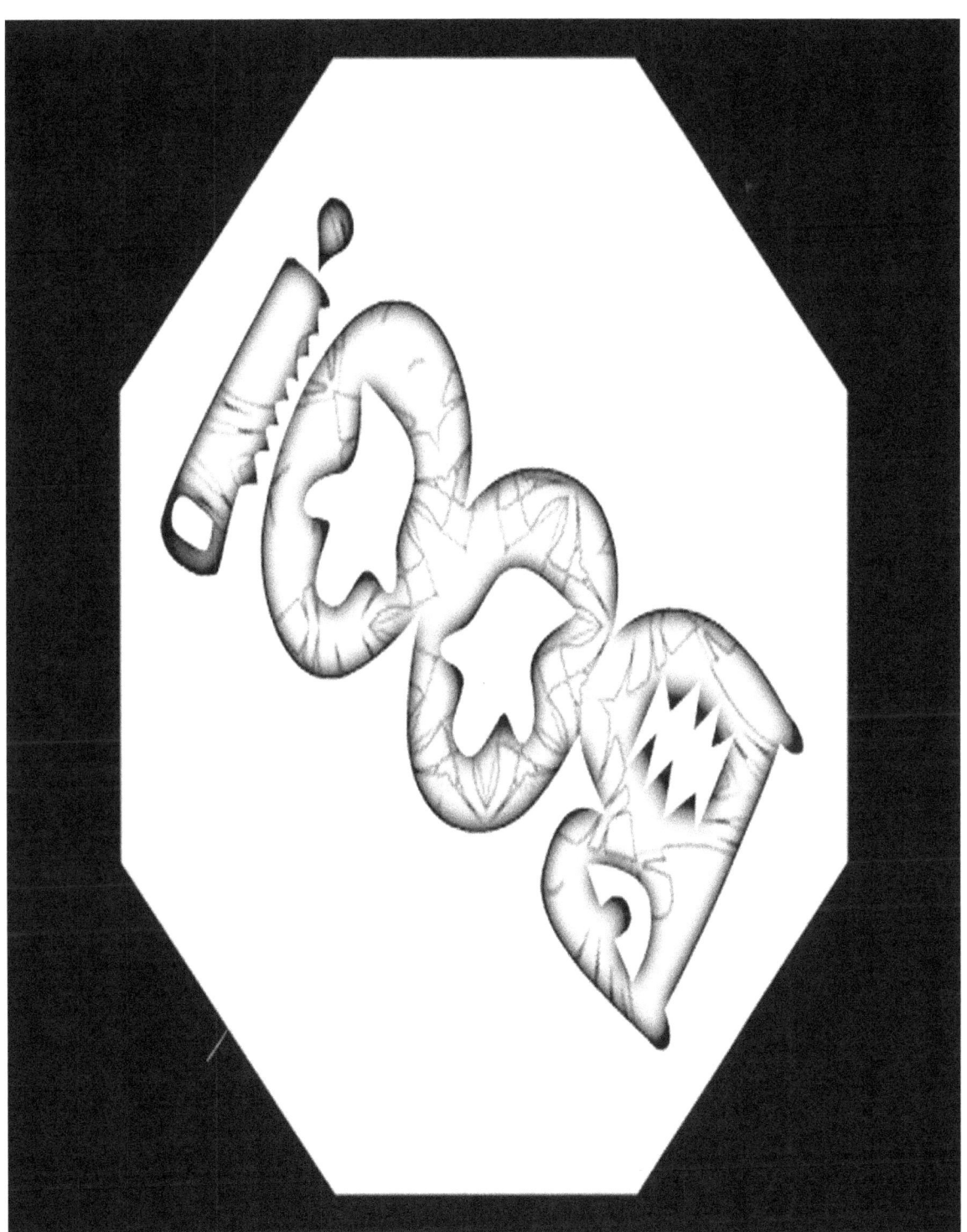

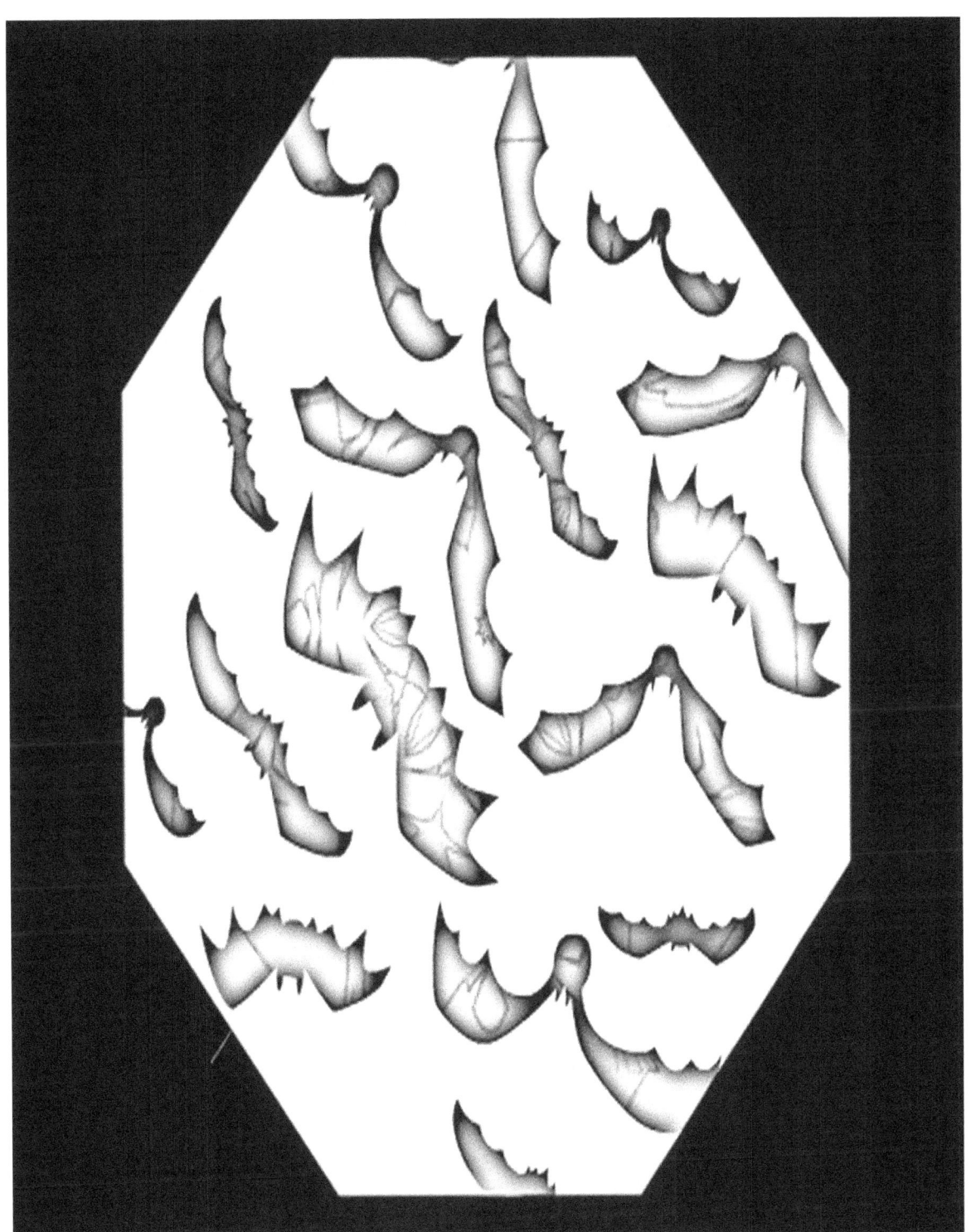

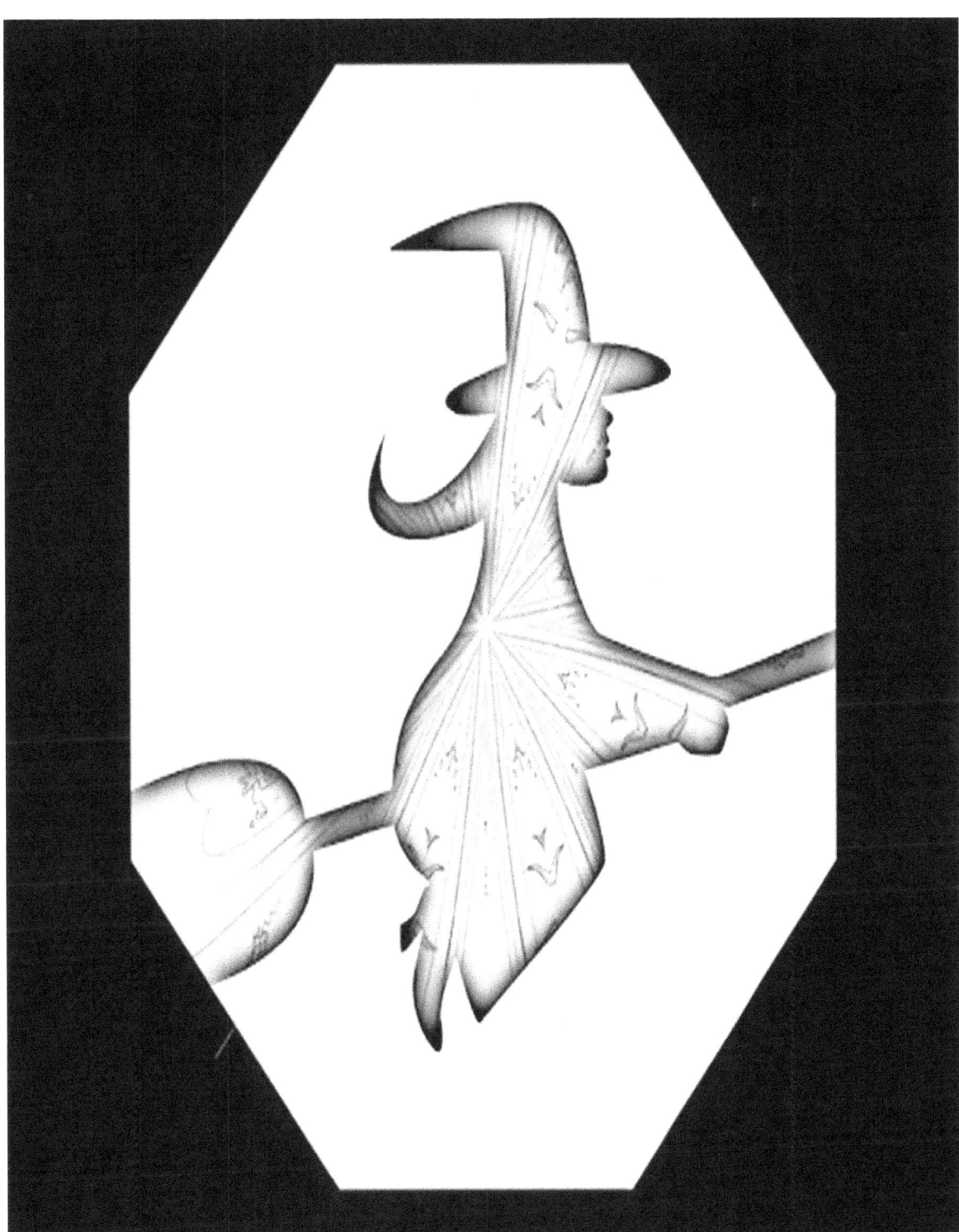

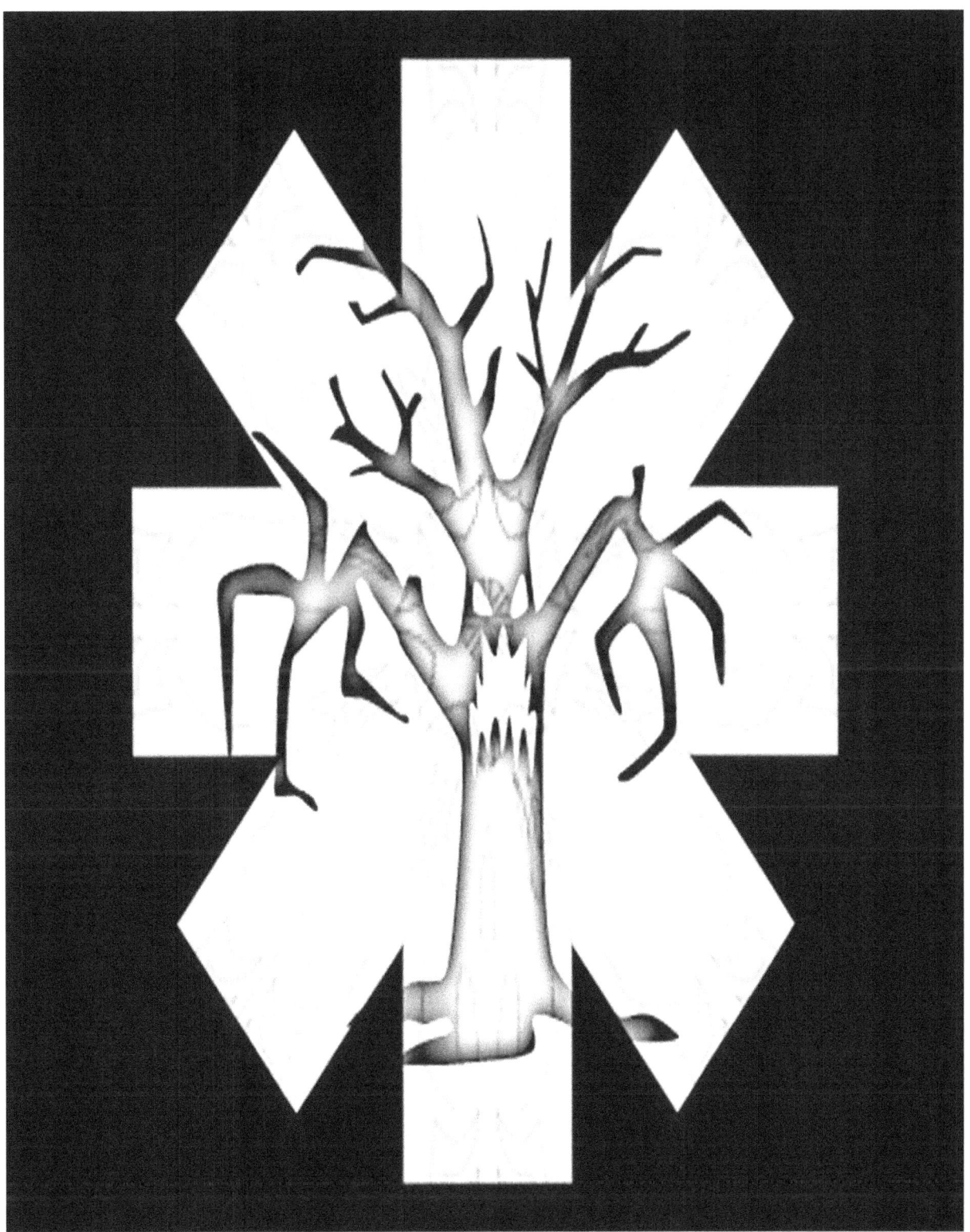

Note